Deep Friendship

Deep Friendship

A Spiritual Journey

GUNILLA NORRIS

Paulist Press
New York / Mahwah, NJ

Cover image by Mario_Hoppmann/Shutterstock.com
Cover design by Sharyn Banks
Book design by Lynn Else

Originally published as *Sheltered in the Heart: Spirituality in Deep Friendship,* copyright © 2015. This new edition copyright © 2026 by Gunilla Norris

Library of Congress Cataloging-in-Publication Data
Names: Norris, Gunilla, 1939– author.
Title: Deep friendship: a spiritual journey / Gunilla Norris.
Other titles: Sheltered in the Heart
Description: New York; Mahwah, NJ : Paulist Press, [2026] | "Originally published as: Sheltered in the Heart: Spirituality in Deep Friendship"—Title page verso. | Summary: "This book is about finding and nurturing that deep spiritual connection between two people"—Provided by publisher.
Identifiers: LCCN 2025022789 (print) | LCCN 2025022790 (ebook) | ISBN 9780809157846 (paperback) | ISBN 9780809189526 (ebook)
Subjects: LCSH: Friendship—Religious aspects. | Interpersonal relations—Religious aspects.
Classification: LCC BL626.33 .N67 2026 (print) | LCC BL626.33 (ebook) | DDC 204/.4—dc23/eng/20250520
LC record available at https://lccn.loc.gov/2025022789
LC ebook record available at https://lccn.loc.gov/2025022790

ISBN 978-0-8091-5784-6 (paperback)
ISBN 978-0-8091-8952-6 (ebook)

Published by Paulist Press
997 Macarthur Boulevard
Mahwah, NJ 07430
www.paulistpress.com

Printed and bound in the
United States of America

In loving memory of
Stanley,
my heart's deep friend

When you love me, I know me better.
When I love you, you know you better.
Within the shelter of love there is
no end to knowing.

Contents

Foreword

I am honored...and also wonderfully perplexed...that Gunilla Norris has asked me to contribute the foreword to her luminous book on spiritual friendship. I am not nearly so confident as she that I will be able to contribute anything to the already exquisite clarity and harmony of her text. I confess to feeling somewhat like a northwesterly gale being invited to blast and rattle my way through a perfectly manicured Japanese garden. I will try my best...big idea process that I am... not to disturb unduly the serenity of the garden.

What Gunilla and I share, beneath some obvious temperamental differences, is our common experience of the path of conscious love...that is, a journey lived deeply and fully with a beloved who is also our closest friend and spiritual companion. It is a path of sheer transparency—grace-filled yet challenging in its complete vulnerability. There is nowhere to hide—for who would want to hide from such love?—but its radiance also turns up the heat on all those personal evasions and shadow behaviors. It is impossible to claim, "I have been misunderstood!!!" I have been understood only too well by one who loves me so much that he or she will settle for nothing less than my full emergence into the divine being I was created to be. In the gentle yet relentless crucible of such love, spiritual transformation happens rapidly, as mortal diamonds soon find themselves ground and polished into "immortal diamonds." For this reason, the path of conscious love—or deep friendship—whichever term speaks more directly to your heart—has been known in the esoteric traditions of the West as "the great cosmic short-cut"; through the solidity of their trust and integrity of their shadow work, the partners soon burn through their karmic deformations and are free to take their place within the luminous freedom-in-unity that is the true nature of love.

Gunilla writes from this place of luminous freedom. She does not write about the experience of transformed love; she writes from it. She does not gossip or sensationalize; she completely end-runs any drama around finding the perfect partner or how to know whether your particular relationship qualifies as a "deep friendship." That's not what the book is about. She even manages, in a wonderfully sly way, to sidestep the whole question of whether the deep friendship needs to be an erotic partnership at all; her gate is wide open to all manner of friendships—gay, straight, celibate, conjugal, filial, imaginal (and I suppose even with pets and houseplants), so long as they are marked by those foundational qualities of stability, transparency, and openness to spiritual growth.

Instead of giving us criteria for measuring and assessing whether our particular friendship qualifies as "deep," she simply assumes that your heart will recognize the real thing if it's on your plate. Sparing no more time on the diagnostics, she instead leads you across the threshold into the real topic, the spiritual attitudes and practices that attend such deep friendships and emerge as the mature fruits of a life lived in such intimate give-and-take.

Each of the short chapters of this book is a profound meditation—etched with Gunilla's haiku delicacy—on the spiritual qualities that both guide the skillful stewardship of such a friendship and emerge over time as its most precious gifts. The qualities she addresses—faithfulness, honesty, compassion, self-acceptance, to name a few—of course the fruits of any mature spiritual life, but when cultivated along the pathway of intimate friendship, they bear a particular sweetness. Gunilla knows this pathway well; clearly, she has fully integrated the gifts of which she speaks, and her words are luminous comfort (as well as wise practical advice) for those of us stumbling our way toward maturity in her footsteps. As I read each meditation—pausing and reflecting as she's requested—I found myself reliving my own relational path, savoring those truths I'd come to discover on my own (mostly through trial and error), and wishing I'd had this book in my hands twenty years ago. It would have allowed me to move so much more confidently and serenely in the direction that love was beckoning.

True lovers, Rilke observes in his *Letters to a Young Poet,* are "two silences that border, protect, and salute one another." To my mind, that quote quintessentially captures the spirit of Gunilla's book, and her wise and compassionate reflections beautifully convey the music of this dance. Her book will be a blessing to all who have begun to discover that spaciousness and intimacy are not opposites; they are the warp and weft of a tapestry whose fullness is Love itself.

Cynthia Bourgeault

Introduction

It's been more than a decade since this book was first published. The subject of spiritual friendship is still vibrant and essential to me. I have been profoundly changed and informed by such friendships. We do not become ourselves without others. The African wisdom of Ubunto declares, "I am because we are." To have a deep, soul friendship is to enter the alchemy of becoming more of who we essentially are. I think of it as holy togethering. Such friendships have helped me to become a person not just an individual with a personality.

How does one explain that? I can't, but I share my reflections here in this book. If you, as the reader, can give yourself to the process, you may experience being worked by love to grow in love so that you can give yourself away. I have been comforted by having a deep friend, and to be one is to be challenged. It is to have a blessing and to be a blessing. It is transformative and, above all, humbling. It requires focus, dedication, self-giving, and two conscious people attending to the movement of love in the depth of their being. In other words, it is spiritual.

Casual friends are people we care about, enjoy, and do things with. We may have many interests in common with such friends. This is true of deeper friendships, too, but in my experience, these friendships have another dimension. They ask us to develop our essence and to grow spiritually. That is something an ordinary friendship might not ask of us.

I cannot define the kind of friendship I am talking about, but I know it is based on love and a connection to Spirit. It has freedom in it and no guarantees. It requires loving awareness and presence. Above all, it is a tender gift that we must live in order to realize.

This book is a collection of reflections culled from many years of dwelling in and caring about this subject. Words will ultimately fail, for deep, spiritual friendship is an experience that contains more than can be articulated. Yet I want to trust that these reflections will bring the reader to examine what it is to have and to be a true friend.

I hope the reader will feel this book to be an invitation, a kind of heart-to-heart conversation that invites us to be open, to consider matters of the most inward kind. I bring up qualities, activities, and attitudes that are helpful in cultivating a deep friendship. As I was writing, I found that an afterthought would come to me. These thoughts are printed in italics to invite a slower pace and an encouragement to reverie. I hope you will mull things over and think about what you have read as your response is integral to this conversation.

Please do not read this book straight through. Let there be time to consider what you would like to add or take exception to. Making space for reflection is often forgotten in our fast-paced society. Let's reclaim the leisure to respond from reverie rather than from rushing.

A loving spiritual connection between people is full of nurturing and waiting. It needs to take place gradually. It is in duration that trust comes into being. Revealing ourselves in depth is fundamentally scary. We can't skip how vulnerable it makes us feel. Yet, as we witness one another's flaws and inner beauty, we are giving and receiving the greatest of gifts. I hope that in reading this book you will find some useful ideas. I hope you will feel encouraged to draw closer to the ground of your own being and to the growth of your spirit. I hope you might give this book to a special person who is or might be trusted to be a true companion on the way.

We are embedded in God's Love. I believe we are asked to develop deep friendships not only for our own sakes but also for the sake of one another and for the sake of Love itself. Together we can attend to the longing that dwells at the core in every one of us and so become more of who we essentially are...part of Love itself.

Gunilla Norris
Westerly, RI
2024

Meeting

When we encounter someone who belongs to our soul's journey, it will happen in an ordinary way and often in a familiar context. Yet it will also happen in a far larger context. Putting words to this is hard because those larger dimensions are so interwoven with our daytime awareness, they are hard to separate. Yet we sense that something significant is happening to us. There is an excitement in the air. We have a sense, even if it is obscure, that we have been found. Something has begun that is vital. Without words we seem to know this. Over time, we will discover how we meet in being, in time, in place, in potential, and in willingness. Over time, we will savor the joys of deep friendship.

BEING

To have a deep friend is to have very special support—yet not as we usually think of support. Such a friend is not a crutch. Such a friend is not someone who will do the inner work we ourselves refuse to do, nor is it someone we hang on to out of loneliness or other unexamined reasons.

Our friend is not to be thought of as either more or less wise than we are. We are both unique and equal. As such, we do not *use* one another. The simple fact that our friend exists at all and is walking his or her path beside us confirms that we are alive in a more than a mundane way. We have a chance to honor the sanctity of each other.

This is a bit like walking in a wood and suddenly coming upon a deer in a glade. Our eyes meet. Our ears prick up. We are exquisitely alert. A special kind of recognition happens. When the deer does not run away, is not frightened, but stays of its own accord on its own business, trusting us and itself to be safe, we feel given to and somehow enlarged. Our natural innocence becomes real. Together we are brought into the purity of simple being. In this light we are simultaneously lifted and illumined.

When two people can be innocent with one another, creature to creature, it is support of a special kind. It allows us to remember that there is within us, at the very core, a sheer and wild perfection.

As deep friends, we shelter the transparent beauty of each other. We protect and value one another in the way an endangered species is valued and protected.

In recognizing the sheer and wild perfection in one another, we understand each other as holy. There will never be another you. There will never be another me.

TIME

If the purity of being is the first place that we meet, then time could be considered the second place. Without convergence how could we find each other? We must meet each other at a specific time. It could happen on a Tuesday in early fall of a particular calendar year. It could be Saturday in spring, two years earlier. It will always be an unrepeatable moment and yet, because *being* is holy, it will also be a timeless moment. We meet simultaneously in infinity and on Tuesday. Feeling and knowing eternity as always with us brings our shared events into the present and into vastness.

Imagine a simple thing like having tea together for instance. The warm vapor from the cups floats up, smoking and curling in the air. It is soundless—a melody. Might we know that we are sipping from the steaming cup of now in the home of forever? The mystery is that in this bit of time when we meet, we also meet everything else. It's hard to remember that.

How much will we be able to drink this in? A sip here and there, and fleetingly at first, but with practice we can taste both worlds at once and drink our fill.

No moment of love is ever lost. Trusting that to be true, we would know that nothing real ever disappears though it changes and continues in some other way. We can't fathom precisely how this is, yet we can trust that it is.

We may be afraid to love because we fear the loss of that love in the future. But are we not both lost and found within the moment's consecration? We are lost because we forget ourselves when we are fully engaged. And we are found again and again in one another's presence.

Living the rich duality of timeliness and timelessness, we become spacious and open. Slowly and with practice, we can come to feel how inclusive and luminous is Now and how radiant is Always.

PLACE

The third way we meet is in the sanctity of place. The Zen saying that no snowflake falls into the wrong place gives us a sound perspective. Wherever we have tumbled is a right place, a holy place despite our propensity to want somewhere better, safer, more exciting, lovelier, and so on. This is especially true when where we are is a cruel and life-threatening situation. Yet even there, given a strong connection to Spirit, we might be able to see our circumstances as part of holy ground.

This is easy to write and searing to live. We meet in *being*, in *time*, and in *place*. Our situations color our experiences very much. A deep friend can be met on a train, in the workplace, on vacation, in a bank or a barrack. We belong to places, even if those places are transient. We cannot be together unless we converge in place and in time.

Now, with the internet, a friend can be met in a placeless place, a virtual space. But sooner or later, we will want to find our friend in the solidity of an actual location. Being human, we need to touch one another, to come together in more than imagination, thought or word.

To meet in the sanctity of place is to honor that we each must have room to be. We are solid and take up space. We are always in a specific somewhere. Wherever that happens to be, it is always our *here*. It is in *place* that we can feel that we are of earth and in mutual connection. It is there that we know that we are *in* the universe and have the universe *within* us.

When we meet at the crossroad, under the clock, at the train station, or by the big oak in the park, we are there solidly as we physically are. Yet we are there in a far bigger way than we can ever know.

Whatever our actual size, we have inner spaces that are immense. There is no way we can be mapped. So why not think of our heart's friend as an expanding universe—filled with galaxies? Then would we not sense that we are vast as well? It is a joy to see the stars in one another.

POTENTIAL

There is another place where we meet. It is in the realm of potential. When two people truly meet, immediately something new happens. We see this easily with children. The moment they have each other's measure and feel secure, they begin to create together both known games and new ones as chance will have it.

As adults, haven't we experienced a sense of empowerment with someone with whom we have affinity? We are awakened to play and to discover. It is as natural as breathing. Brought close to one another, two smoldering logs in a fireplace catch heat from one another and begin to burn more brightly. An existing and vital potential is brought out in both. The energy is evident. Whenever we sense capacity in another, we are natural catalysts and become agents of encouragement. This is always the case when we are lucky to find someone who resonates with our being.

How wonderful it is then to look upon one another as bearers of inspiration and potential! This way of seeing can become a habit of welcome, a great courtesy of heart. And when we are also perceived this way, there is a new spring to our step, a sense of possibility that supports us.

It is good to know that to be a true friend of even one person is a lifetime's opportunity. The heart's journey is too deep to share with more than a very few. Such a chance may be rare, but when it comes, a fire starts in which much can be forged.

We are ignited, tempered, and warmed. We see the world with new eyes and are born—both carried along and given birth to what we have the potential to become.

WILLINGNESS

Another inexplicable meeting place is in the attitude of willingness—the convergence of instinct and feeling. Why we are willing to be suddenly and freely open to another human being is a complete mystery. The people we travel in depth with can be so different from our usual connections. Why our heart simply says *yes*, we will not know. But could we not suspect that such openings are not chance but Spirit at work...that we are brought together for a reason beyond mere liking or curiosity? Are we not to form something, to become something in association with that other, who is precisely the one who needs us as we need them?

Such travel companions do not have to be companions for life, though they can become that. They are not necessarily our spouses or our best friends. As companions on the way, they enter our journey with significance, and our hearts are flung open.

When we think of the most important events of our lives, they are usually not constructed. They happen in a moment, in a place, out of simply being who we are. In the excitement of recognition we say, *Yes.* This yes is not from the mind but from a place that lies beyond our ken. Could we say that we enter into a kind of response—ability to and for one another? It is as if we were mysteriously brought to a trailhead to begin a journey. We do not know where the path may lead, only that Spirit has opened a way for us both.

We usually sense affinity at once, but it can also happen with someone with whom we initially have little in common, who in time is revealed to be a deep friend. The fact dawns on us slowly.

Many small events are needed before a match is struck and we find our hearts kindled. Moments of knowing can never be planned. They are given to us. Our responding "yes" is given to us as well. We cannot conjure or command it. We can only recognize it and then gratefully receive it.

Such a response is spontaneous—a gift and an opening. We know we are living a significant and fiery moment.

Understanding

We all long to be understood. Fundamentally, this is not about agreeing, though that seems to make things appear easier. But understanding is much deeper than that. It is a profound spaciousness that grants another person the chance to be known from their own perspective and revealed in their history, their joys, their sorrows, their struggles and strengths. When we really understand one another that way, it is like making a beautiful ring of support. The jewel of the self is given a setting in which to be held and seen. It is one of the dearest parts of friendship.

THE PAST

When we embrace the sanctity in each other, we have a foundation on which much can be built. We naturally want to understand more about what has made us who we are. That is the stuff of intimacy. It deepens and enlarges our connection.

Does it matter that our friend knows where we were born, what our family was like, what schools we attended, what places we lived in, who we loved in the past? The answer is *no*. We do not need to know these things to feel and honor the sanctity in one another.

Yet even casual friends want to know a little about each other. It is natural in a friend to know many of those particulars. In a deep friendship, such things are important but not in a classifying way. Our histories have shaped us, but we are not defined by them.

We don't want to know things about each other so as to categorize, summarize, or define one another. Knowing each other's past is simply background. The foreground is our moment-to-moment experience.

Taking distance from our past, we are like birds flying over a terrain. We can feel the thermals rising from the territory of the past. We are warmed and lifted by some of them, and some suck us down. Strong wings are needed to bear up. Side by side we help gain perspective and understanding. It is very hard to observe ourselves clearly on our own. Without a loving other, it is almost impossible to know who we are.

Sharing our past is a sacred trust. It is not casual. In a deep friendship, we can trust that our histories will never be used against us. When we remember together, we reconstruct the body of our past. We gain perspective and often reassurance.

We also discover unresolved pain, and it is not so much what happened to us that is as important as how we responded to what happened. Our histories carry the facts, but it is how we experienced those facts, and what we did with them, that will reveal who we really are.

Giving each other heartfelt acceptance opens us to more self-acceptance.

JOYS

Revisiting the past is a bit like looking at a marked map. We know the sequence of where and when things happened. We can trace the path we once traveled. But entering the territory of memory, we will no longer be *above* events; we will be *in* them. Recollection allows us to re-experience.

Memories are often changed slightly when we share them with someone we trust. Together we open to more knowing and feeling. For some, sharing past joys is more poignant than sharing past pain. When we recall the joys of our early life, we are no longer looking at a map, we are in the territory of experience. We are both living *now* and re-living *then*, and have access to our youthful sense of things, the vivid *such-ness* of the world.

The taste, smell, and touch of goodness, when shared with another, will be present once again. In the eyes of our friend we will know, not only that joy happened to us, but that the capacity for it is still alive and well in us. For each of us there is a pattern which consistently gives us joy.

Early joys are very powerful. We know what touched us though we can't explain the sense of kinship with it. Nurtured, planted, and given roots, early joys are soul seeds that remain alive in us until the end of our lives.

Memories slip in and out. Though we might not easily remember it, something germane continues from our early years—a wonder, a knowing, a particular way to fall in love with the world.

When we know something about it, we can further one another. Remembering and cultivating joy is not frivolous. It is a spiritual fire which when it burns can bring us into our true work in the world.

With a loving friend, we can discover early seeds of joy that still guide our choices in life, and if these joys are not yet lived, we can help each other to bring them into life so that we can embody them.

Joy is a mark of the Spirit. We express joy when we live what allows us to feel who we essentially are.

SORROWS

Whenever we remember our joys, we cannot help but remember our sorrows as well. They are tied together. When we remember the one, the other seems also to be pulled out of the past into present awareness. This is so because, by its nature, joy includes all that is not yet within its compass.

Inner joy unlike happiness is not dependent on circumstance. It is a condition of being—a profound acceptance of pathos. Could we dare to say that joy is not joy unless sorrow has found a home within it? That can change how we look upon our grief. Accepted, it becomes the royal road to that transcendent place of knowing life as it really is—sweet, bitter, and true. Sorrows refine us. Embracing them, our souls grow. The dross is burned out of us when we submit to the fire. As the alloys—our preferences and insistences—melt away, we can begin to feel how everything, even dreadful things can carry meaning and forge us into wholeness.

Sharing one another's sorrows is a tender aspect of deep friendship. We should not be so ready to be rid of our grief when it is the very path to the heart. Together we realize that sorrows fully accepted mark our faces. We seem to shine with wisdom when we are able to witness this in each other. We acknowledge a sense of wholeness, a realized strength in our bearing.

Whenever any sorrow is taken fully to heart, we learn something profound. A window opens where a door is closed.

The soul expands. Assumptions about ourselves are shed. We become naked to actual experience, and so more joined to the world.

We know how easy it is to fall into self-pity or into pity for another. But the loving thing is to see one another as being capable of whatever comes our way. If we do not refuse our sorrows and kiss them instead, will they not become beautiful? Wouldn't the world glitter through our tears as the sun does after rain?

STRUGGLES

There are forces that defeat us, perhaps must defeat us, so that we can somehow become fuller persons. Could we think of these challenges as angels we must wrestle until we gain a blessing from them as Jacob did in the Old Testament? Deep friends can help each other here. We want to complain when things are tough, and we strategize to overcome whatever is in our way. But if we could ask each other what the inherent blessing is in what is difficult, we would be better served.

Not for a moment are we to skirt over the grit, sweat, and pain of challenges, but we can see them as other than useless pain. If we could consider them somehow as worthy forces, then our struggles with them would have dignity. We might lose many battles, but we would not lose our connection to Spirit. How would we know anything about ourselves without such angels? Wouldn't we remain untested, untried, and somehow never reach spiritual maturity?

Tests in life inevitably come. If we wallow in our difficulties and use our precious energy in complaint, we will merely become victims. If we grin and bear them or deny our challenges, we are not living truthfully. We are numbed. If we are fighting someone else's battle, we often rob them of their chance for resolution and dignity. It is only when the challenge is truly ours, and when we give our all, that both victory and defeat become less important. It is then we are asking for a blessing and not an outcome.

As we share when and how we have suffered, could we listen without pity? Could we help each other and not enable each other, taking the time to consider what is truly of help?

Let us not assume we know for a fact. With patience, we lend our presence as our friend grapples. Tempted to intervene, we can remember that the struggle belongs to our friend and is not ours.

This is true in reverse. We must trust each other to be capable of wrestling with our angels. To trust this way is reverent. Misguided help can be worse than no help. Let us be the help that supports both dignity and endurance.

STRENGTHS

Struggles seem to be matched with strengths the way joy is matched with sorrow. We are not tested everywhere. Our struggles are usually particular to our character. When we meet our difficulties without shirking, we become more of who we really are. There is a curious mercy here because we usually do not get more than we can bear. And when we bear whatever we must to its fullest, to term, we give birth to something new in ourselves—a larger capacity of being.

Strength is often thought of as might, endurance, or some form of force. But spiritually speaking, strength is the great art of not fighting against what *is* but engaging it with all our heart. Sometimes that amounts to a fortitude that allows things to be or to develop without our insistence. Perhaps inner strength is a kind of mother love. It holds difficulty like a baby and looks for what is needed rather than for what is wanted. Held in such tender awareness, we are also held back from precipitous action.

When we understand our lives better, we can see where such strength was at work. Always a gift given by Spirit, it is a surprise to us that we were able to prevail. It is often *after the fact* that we discover we have been given the gift of strength.

A true friend can give us encouragement by knowing our history, our joys and our sorrows, our struggles and our strengths, and in their eyes, we can see ourselves better.

What one person carries easily, another person cannot bear. We join strength with strength. A single stick is easily broken. Two sticks together are harder to snap. Together we bear our own and each other's burdens better, and we understand when the other must go it alone.

Sometimes holding is simply the ability to see a bigger picture. Sometimes holding is support and nurturing help, and sometimes holding is stepping back and letting things be. In retrospect, the latter is often sensed as profound help, though in the present we might feel it as counterintuitive. We are, after all, still present for one another though we are not "doing anything."

Deep friends know they are trusted to handle their own challenges in their own way and in their own timing.

Honesty

The mind has many tricks. It can fool us. On the one hand, we can name what we believe to be true while, on the other hand, we can hide what we are ashamed of or not capable of facing at a given time. It is not uncommon to make separate compartments for different aspects of our actions and thoughts. Even to be aware that we have denials takes great courage. Honesty requires much emotional nakedness and vulnerability. In contrast to the mind, a loving heart has a greater capacity to hold our shadow and unformed knowing. The witness that a friend brings to us with such an open heart can help us in the great work of becoming true to ourselves. Together we can gain clarity, sort priorities, face our faults, understand the vows we have made and keep to our devotion.

CLARITY

By understanding the issues we each grapple with, we help each other gain clarity. No problems are solved until they are identified. No goals are reached until they are named. Within a relationship of trust and love, we have the assurance of honesty and the generosity of presence that help us sort things out.

Everyone faces challenges and issues—those places where decisions are made, and character is revealed. Identifying what is going on at any given time is a first step. It requires that we love one another not only with our hearts but also with our minds. During an issue, we might not know what is happening. As we clarify, there is a sifting that goes on—a bit like using a sieve at the beach. There is always so much extraneous stuff that must pass through for us to be able to see the stones that block the flow—the stumbling blocks at the bottom of it all.

Together we can let the sand run and see what remains. Clarifying what is in the way of our path is a form of mutual intercession. When we try to do this alone, we often have doubts and tend to second-guess ourselves. Together we create a stronger understanding of the truth and gain the confidence that, though we do not yet have solutions, we are making clear what belongs to us to deal with. Isn't wisdom often just this—the patience to allow for extraneous issues to empty out and so reveal what is left for us to face and deal with honestly?

How we sort colors our future solutions. Identifying things in fear or judgment makes them enemies. Clarifying them as mere facts of life may be pragmatic but may also lack feeling. Naming with spunk, naming with humor—all color our future solutions.

Could we not only learn to be honest about our issues, but also realize how we sense and feel them? This brings us into a fuller knowledge of the tasks before us and what can be changed for the better.

An issue may not be so daunting in and of itself. The difficulty may lie in how we think and feel about it. When we are able to tease each other or encourage each other, it is as if we put a tinted gel over a spotlight. The stage we then see goes from something drab and dark to a more colorful set where new acts can begin.

PRIORITIES

When beset by whatever challenges us, we not only have to be honest about the problem and our attitude toward it, we must also set priorities for handling both the circumstance and the feelings we have. We might ask: *What is most chronic? What must be handled first? Can it be handled first?* Helping one another to set goals and priorities is like making a trip-tick for a journey.

We may not know entirely where we want to go, or must go, but we have at least clarified where we are. In doing so, we have opened the possibility of traveling on several roads. Sometimes it may be that the priority we come to is no action at all—just days of rest or time needed for the nothing we never allow ourselves.

In a deep friendship where one of us cannot see the priority, the other is often able to do so. Where one of us is still pushing the gas pedal, the other may know to steer us into a rest stop. Our heart's friend may also be able to see that we cannot do something alone or should not.

There are so many things that determine where we find ourselves. So many roads have converged to the specific spot on our life's map where we happen to be now. It's there that we have an opportunity to decide what we are about, what must be left behind, what must be left dormant and what, even very small things, can change the whole nature of our journey.

We can never take for granted the gift that setting priorities is.

We travel together in so many ways, and we may even end up at the same destination, but we have different ways to order what is important to each of us. Sharing our priorities when neither of us is in stress or distress is a wonderful thing.

It is then we learn how we order what is important to us just for the fun of knowing.

If we are ever in an urgent moment of having to choose, it is then that we will be able to remind each other of what matters most to each other.

Having a deep friendship can be a priority in and of itself, though there will be times when we cannot act on it. Still, we can feel that we are there with each other and for each other.

We can also accept that our heart's friend must sometimes take a road away from us until it is possible to come together again.

FAULTS

To be honest about our faults in the presence of love takes guts. It is healing to name our failings and unhelpful habits of being. It is important to have no illusions about ourselves either in detriment or in self-assigned grandeur. We are so very human, of the earth—a kind of humus, and from a larger perspective, very humorous, too. Really, how important do we think we are?

When the friend of our heart still loves us despite our worst faults, we can learn to love ourselves better. To be revealed with the limps of character we each have is very naked, indeed. Most likely, this is the humus that we must work with all our lives. We may improve a little, but the tendencies to anger, impatience, discouragement, grandiosity, delusion, lack of courage, and so on, are there, mixed in with our positive qualities.

Perhaps we are born with these inherent tendencies. Perhaps our intrinsic goodness and our innate faults are meant to meet day by day so as to become something new and whole? Then who would we most want to have in our corner if not our heart's friend who honors the whole process with us? Who, but our friend, will be our sometime catalyst, confidant, confessor, and consoler?

In a museum any bronze statue with an unusual body part, such as a big nose or a humpback, seems to get touched more than others. Hand after hand strokes the nose, the back, the giant toe.

It is uncanny how these symbolic faults are recognized. We probably touch them with a subtle recognition that we all have faults, even if they are internal and not on display.

No museum guard is fast enough to stop these quick caresses. Little by little the metal starts to lighten up, and in time it begins to glisten.

Could it be that in recognizing and caressing the unwanted truth, new light comes through—in fact, must come through?

VOWS

It can be easier to be honest about our goals and priorities than to be honest about our vows. Vows are a different order of commitment. We don't state priorities when we marry, enter a religious order, or commit our lives to something. We take vows. They are intentions of a greater magnitude. We take them in front of others to be witnessed by them and to have their support. We know a vow needs to be made with our whole being, for once decided upon and witnessed, our lives will be profoundly changed. It is a promise made to us and to Spirit.

A vow can be thought of as a spine. It holds us up; it holds us together. To break it is to break apart. To make a vow is to name the commitment to something or to someone and to the loneliness such a commitment entails. Vows are up to us to keep and to us alone. No one can live them for us.

Sometimes we do not know that we have taken a vow. It is secret, unwitnessed and hidden in our unconscious. *I will never again…or I must always….* We made vows such as these when we were vulnerable and immature. Such vows are often made not to be *for* something, but to protect us from future hurt. Hidden vows are sometimes the ones that prevent us from making the life-giving ones that complete and fulfill us.

As deep friends, could we uncover the vows that are unconscious and detrimental in our lives? Together we might then also find the new vows we can make, the ones that bring us into full personhood.

As deep friends, we see how we live and so can ask those questions that cause us to be more and more truthful. Are we living with and for our vows? Can we be honest about what matters to us? Without mutual witnessing we may not ever come to know what we are living for.

In a vow it seems that bliss and challenge are always paired. Do we accept both? Challenged—our backs to the wall—we are stretched to the utmost for the sake of our heart's promise. We suffer it and often that very suffering is the portal to meaning and to our bliss.

There is a loneliness imbedded in the making and the keeping of a vow. As we live our dedication, we witness each other's aloneness, and it helps keep our spines straight. We back each other up.

DEVOTION

Can we honestly name what we worship? Who is God for us? We know God cannot in reality be named, for naming, even as it reveals also conceals. The Mystery that is God has no limits and cannot be defined. And yet, we know the profound human need to call God by name. The names of God are continually and infinitely revealed and revered in countless ways: Companion, Love, Justice, Peace, Grace, Fruition, Beauty, Redemption, Forgiveness—on and on goes the naming as aspects of God become numinous for us.

What name of God is central to us? Being honest about how God touches us, we can better worship together. If we understand our friend's devotion to an aspect of God, we can honor it and be honored in return.

Many traditions chant a sacred name in relation to an aspect of God. What name would sing in our hearts and call us to daily remembrance? This may change at different times in our lives. Where Justice might once have been the name we felt most drawn to in our relationship to God, it may be that Mercy becomes what we grow into in later years.

This can be fierce territory. We know dreadful wars have been fought over which name is the true and only name for God. Could we remember that at the core in each of us is God, the unnamed Presence, who whispers *our* name in a still small voice? That name is for us to hear. It is for us to become.

We worship gods we do not recognize as such. They are hidden. We respond to them automatically, compelled somehow to turn toward them in devotion. Addictions are like that whether to substances, activities, or habits of thought and emotional leanings.

Once triggered, we give ourselves to these inauthentic gods looking for something to shield us from fear, uncertainty, or boredom.

Could we be honest about what enslaves us? In doing so, we might be able to stop our unconscious devotion to illusory gods and turn instead to the One in whom we really live and move and have our being.

Being honest about our faults, our priorities, our vows, and our devotion, could we come to know that we are already in the awesome mystery of God's love where we are called by name?

Faithfulness

Faithfulness requires presence and awareness more than we might ever think. It is not static, a one-time decision we make. Faithfulness is a continuous process with daily attendance and care. It requires that we grow beyond the present moment because life will inevitably bring us tensions and conflicts to address. We will have to declare where we say yes and where we must draw a line and say no. To be faithful, we must discriminate and adhere to our deepest intuitions and commitments. Not only in our quiet, contemplative times when we intercede for one another, but also in the hubbub of daily activities, faithfulness is a lived prayer. It demands that we become trustworthy for the sake of our heart's dear friend and for the depth of our being.

TENSION

A profound characteristic of a deep friendship is that it is faithful. This means a quality of presence that can be counted upon over time. It means an innocence of heart that remains open even through difficult times. It means a trust that whatever befalls us, our friendship can be understood to be about mutual development. In the marriage ceremony, we say, "*for better or for worse*." In a consecrated friendship, we might say, "*in trust that Spirit is taking us deeper into life*."

Faithfulness is a virtue that can tolerate disappointment and difficulty. It makes us real in a three-dimensional way. It makes us human persons instead of mere individuals. Faithfulness is not some kind of blind acquiescence and acceptance of one another. Faithfulness has muscle. It has duality built into it, for we need to be faithful to our own inner truth as well as to support the truth of our friend. This may challenge us to be true in opposite directions. In that tension, the new in both of us can be born.

The ability to bear tension with vigor and equanimity is what makes music of relatedness. Think of a guitar and how its strings must be fastened at two ends and must be strung to a bearing pitch. It is only possible in that condition to play the instrument and to sound a true note.

In a deep friendship, we cannot escape that our hearts must be tuned frequently. We will be asked to confront one another at times, to say *yes* and *no* clearly and to love each other through conflicting desires.

On the one hand, we lean into and trust the faithfulness of our heart's friend. On the other hand, we attend to our mutual commitment as if it needed constant tuning. What a paradox! Trust and watchful attentiveness—it seems they would cancel each other out.

A dual aspect of a muscle is that it contracts and expands. Like any muscle, faithfulness can only lift and carry if it is used. Contracting and expanding, we learn the mysteries of deep companionship. Then, whatever inner growth happens belongs to the both of us.

SAYING *NO*

Spiritual friends do not enable one another—we ennoble each other instead. There is genuine carefulness in our interactions, and because that is true, it is more vital that we are able to say *no.* This can seem counterintuitive.

Let's suppose that, in a given moment, we have conflicting desires. One of us needs the other to be available for talk and comfort, and the other needs at that same moment to be alone. How does one say *no* either to one's own desire or to the desire of the other? It requires that we feel the tension, and that we refuse to go into an automatic response.

Could we ask what would ennoble the relationship—what would honor the tensile strength of it? We can only find out by finding out. If we can pause long enough to feel the heart's capacity to hold disparate things, we would say our *no* in such a way that we do not reject the other—or feel rejected by the other—and remain in our integrity.

Then we embrace the entire situation, not just our own particular part of it. We say our *no* from a stretched heart. A gentle *no* is so much more loving than an acquiescing *yes.* We will feel the considerations that go into the answers we give. We can feel the honoring of both self and other, and the trust that we have in our friend not to take offense.

There may be many times we might feel disappointed by each other's *no,* but that is far different from experiencing rejection.

We can practice saying no. There are many available moments for a kind no. *If we practiced apart from our friendship, our comfort with* no *might become easier. We might begin by smiling at habits we want to change and say a loving* no *to them.*

Perhaps this could be no *to a second helping of food or no to avoiding doing the taxes, or* no *to a solicitor on the phone. Each one becomes practice. We might begin to like no more than we ever thought we could. Our no might become gentler and yet more penetrating and truthful. It might enter the hidden pockets of avoidance and cowardice that each of us has.*

Our lives would become cleaner and our love more visible. When we say no *to someone, they are allowed to see where we stand.*

SAYING *YES*

How easy it is to say *yes* when the heart is open and connected! It's as easy as breathing. Fundamentally, we want to say *yes* to life, to love, and to committed work. The trouble is that we are prone to say too many *yeses*.

Just as a considered *no* clears the way for a considered *yes*, so a considered *yes* implies many *nos* for life to come into order and integrity. This is as demanding in a close friendship as it is elsewhere in life, though it tends to get muddier there, since we feel deeply drawn toward our friends.

For instance, isn't it better to see each other a little less, if when we are face-to-face, our *yes* is imbued with a quality of full presence? Another example might be that we take the time to discern where we can help the other the most and let smaller giving impulses go unattended.

To receive is a *yes* and takes vital energy also. When we are habitual givers, we forget what that might mean to the one who is to receive what we habitually give. If what is given is on the mark, we receive easily and openly. In other circumstances, let's admit that receiving can be work.

With *yes* and *no*, our way unfolds. Unless we are aware, we simply react instead of acting mindfully. Within the opportunity of a conscious friendship, this could be a wonderful area to explore. We would learn how profound is a *no* or a *yes*. They are the breath of giving and receiving.

What if on a chosen day we thought of placing our no in the left, more subordinate hand, and our yes in the right, more dominant hand? The left hand and arm are closer to the heart. Might we with this little game grant our body's heart side the task of saying no and our right more discriminating side the task of being openhanded and saying yes?

The usual circuits would get switched. Our bodies may sense something differently than what our minds know. Then when we use both hands to engage the world with a no or a yes, a different quality of experience is likely. We may feel our choices more fully.

Daily we discriminate with yes and no. In our special friendships, could we help one another to be not only faithful but evenhanded?

CONFLICT

Even in the deepest and most chosen relationships, conflicts arise. Our points of view collide in some unsolvable way. *Yes* finds only *no* and vice versa. We feel distraught with the very person with whom we would like to be constant.

The tendency, when things are so, is to try *to solve* the rupture instead of embracing it. Giving in to each other is not what deep friends should make a practice of.

Real differences of opinion that lead us to choices away from each other become those opportunities to increase what love and commitment are all about. When we draw a circle and declare that within its precinct we can be in accord, we limit our world. How freeing it is when we make that circle either bigger or something entirely else—a space where opposite points of view can still be in relationship. To agree to disagree can lead us to new ideas of what is possible.

The open hand of love lets go and remains open. In conflict, we learn to allow some primal fears simply to be: fear that we will lose our friendship and so be abandoned; fear that we will be asked to live something we cannot or will not live; fear that we are not able to perform what the other needs or wants; fear that our resources will not be sufficient, and more.

Simply put, we must give fear time and space and kindness. To remain faithful amid misunderstanding is more proof of love than any quick patch up that lets us out of a sticky place.

Misunderstandings are not as specific as we make them out to be. They carry moods and usually a past that may have nothing to do with the present. We may need to look for where and when we had similar difficulties in our history—ones we have brought unknowingly to the present.

We can realize that this is also true for our friend. We must rely on patience and kindness to give us time for understanding. Emotional space, mutually given, is an enormous gift. We can understand that something larger than is apparent is happening to us both.

When our friend gives us time and does not close the door on us, we can feel how we are still joined despite the bumps in the road. Together we can continue to grow into lighter and lighter beings.

PRAYER

An obvious aspect of faithfulness between deep friends is that we pray for each other. When we need and ask for prayer, we might hear people say, *I hold you in the Light,* or *I hold you in heart and mind.*

We are glad of that, of course. But what about holding each other in the Light for no good reason at all and for the best reason—to be faithful? Do we allow ourselves the experience that we are supported by one another's prayerfulness?

Mostly, we note it mentally as a nice thing, but we often don't take the time to incorporate the fact—take it into our body. Could we not only pray *for* each other daily but also take the time *to receive* those prayers?

Prayer is substantial and has both weight and direction. It has heat, strength, and duration. In prayer, we are given more than we can ever digest or understand. Prayer may not always cure what ails us, but it is a comfort and takes us further spiritually. Prayer, for and with each other, is a profound conviction that Love is taking place and that we, in our smallness, are tapping into the very immensity that created the universe. Sacred writings amply testify that we can experience this.

Beyond conflict and tension, beyond the *yeses* and *nos* of our lives, when we place our heart's friend in the radiant mystery of God's love and remain with them there in trust, we do one of the most faithful things we can do as companions on the way.

When we pray for our friend, we are also incorporated into the prayer because prayer is a dynamic give-and-take. We are mutually infused and re-created in profound and subtle ways. As deep friends, we will be able to verify this as our lives unfold.

Sometimes we will feel the sending of prayer more, at other times, the receiving. But in the end, sending and receiving tend to merge. There is no sender and no receiver. There is just prayer happening.

We could decide ahead of time to be at prayer at a specific time and feel that we are together though physically we might be miles apart. We know how electricity runs a computer as well as a toaster. Love, like an electric current, flows into our friendship when we connect to it, and then we are given energy in ways we individually need and much more besides.

Compassion

It is easy for us to pity others. It doesn't cost us much. When we pity, we are safely away from any real, deep participation in suffering. Compassion, however, asks us to respond from our viscera. To be in each other's lives with compassion means that we are in a profound participatory comprehension. It is about being truly human together. We extend the balm of empathy to one another instead of feeling sorry for each other. We learn to be balanced and useful in the presence of difficulty. We offer the stability of companionship when it is needed, and together our lives take part in the larger context of community. So intimate is compassion that it brings the world and its wounds into our very breath. We know that each of us is *because we all are.*

BALM

Compassion is that stirring of the heart that lets us participate with others in the trials of life. Without it, our world would be very cold. Sorrows that are shared are more bearable. Carried with another, they become means of transformation and transcendence. In them and through them, we bond as we hold each other in empathic understanding.

Compassion allows us to know we are not isolated, not forgotten or alone. Whether we are giving or receiving it, the very fact that another knows where we are is like coming out of darkness. Compassion is not only seeing the truth with our minds, but it is also feeling it fully. This is participatory knowing. We are brought out of isolation when someone feels with us but does not identify with us.

This is profound and hard to explain. To feel another's difficulty of whatever nature without becoming enmeshed with them is a great act of awareness. On the receiving end of this equation, we can sense that we are lovingly witnessed rather than emotionally entangled. Then our own tears become significant and real to us. We taste the salt in them. We feel their wet presence on our faces. We *real*ize them as ours.

Together we know that, in the depths of pain, Spirit is at work. With each other's compassion, we can be more vulnerable and undefended. It is a great balm. The path is not *around* but *through* what life brings. With each other's empathy, we are able to live what we must and dare to feel all of it.

The dictionary's definition of empathy is: "an imaginative projection of one's own consciousness into another's being." We can only imagine the suffering that our friends are undergoing, and so our responses cannot be as mirrors that reflect just what is in front of us. Our responses to suffering will be colored and shaped by our own experience.

Though we will never fully feel or exactly understand the suffering of a friend, we are more alike as human beings than we are different. We can hope that the mutuality our friends feel from us covers the mistakes we might make in responding to their pain.

PITY

Compassion is not pity, yet it often masks that emotion. Pity has a hierarchical quality. We are above or distanced from what we pity. We are perhaps even secretly disapproving of that which is being pitied. We can also be afraid of it, so we cover our fear with a mask of pity. We are then feeling "for" another with secret superiority or with relief that we have escaped the fate we are observing. These are but two examples of how we might be distancing ourselves from someone for whom we feel we ought to have empathy.

This is subtle and degrading to both parties. When we pity, we are often simply avoiding pain and will give money, advice, and personal efforts to not feel what we imagine the other to be feeling. In compassion, we behave quite differently. It isn't that we are only trying to feel what the other person feels or to rescue them from their fate. It is that we are willing to be present with the ones we love in their pain and with our own discomforts about their pain without masking anything.

Often, we don't have such maturity. But when we are able to do this—even a little—it is experienced as a gift. We sense that our heart's friend has not dismissed us in do-goodness, in subtle judgment, or in rescue operations of one kind or another. We sense they are there *with* us—love with love, fear with fear—helplessness with helplessness—joined in the vulnerability and mystery of being human. In that sense of solidarity, the heart cracks wide open and lets Spirit in.

We can't do compassion. We can only be it. In compassion, our friend's pain, and the suffering we feel witnessing that pain, merges as one. Relieving suffering where we can is natural, yet we are not to mask pain or take it away, for we learn much in it and through it.

Could we be near one another when we suffer and allow each other to experience what we must without avoidance? When we do that, we give to each other in an immense way. Together we are able to be in the hells that sometime happen in life and still feel we have light.

BALANCE

To sustain compassion is difficult when there are chronic conditions such as ill-health or sustained losses. Such continuous experiences are hard on both parties, and learning to have compassion for oneself in such situations is a necessity.

In the face of pain, feeling sorry for oneself or the opposite—ignoring or suppressing oneself—are all efforts at management. We know management isn't compassion. It is control and efficiency. Could we imagine a seesaw—one end will go up if there is enough weight to make the opposite side go down? Feeling anger, pity, or resentment will tip the balance. The heavy side goes down and throws much up in the air.

Ignoring our own feelings and needs is a deadweight also, though we might not know it. Down goes the seesaw and up goes disconnection and distraction.

A loved friend's loss or difficulty will make an impact on us, and because it does, it is even more incumbent on us to find the inner balance that lets us live in and with things as they are. When we neither ignore what is happening nor feel victimized by it, we find a middle ground where the big swings of feeling can be balanced. A compassion that is lived has an objective center. It helps us be with pain without identifying with it. Able to witness pain, feel it and not merge with it, we are spacious and have left reactivity behind for Love's sake.

Anxiety and fear vibrate in our bodies. They are fast emotions and stir up our nervous systems. We feel antsy and scattered. These emotions send urgent signals to find immediate solutions. It is exactly here that we need compassion. When everything cries out for action, we can sit in the center of it all allowing thought and emotion to come to balance and turn from reactivity and management into real feeling—a place of integration where we can dangle our legs into uncertainty and still relax.

Not trapped by reactivity, we know that solutions are hidden within our problems. We also understand that sometimes there are no solutions—things will not change for the better. We must accept them as they are.

COMPANIONSHIP

As companions, we remind each other that we are always living within the context of a vast Love that suffers in us and through us. We exist in a continuous Compassion. As we turn our suffering over to that Love, something profound happens to us.

Often the circumstances have not changed nor have our own discomforts, but we can sense an inner strength, a knowledge that nothing of our experience is skipped over or dismissed as valueless. Our suffering has both purpose and meaning.

No longer will we identify ourselves as victims nor gloss over the difficulties we find ourselves in. It is in conscious suffering that Love is present. Together in that mystery we feel our vulnerability transformed into something luminous.

This can be practiced when small afflictions befall us. Feeling a "*poor me*" coming on, we remind each other to invite the loving presence of Spirit and to remember we are not alone. Shared suffering is shared truth and opens us to more acceptance. In practicing this, we are not anticipating terrible things. On the contrary, we are learning to be inwardly free. In small, daily practices we make a habit of being free no matter what.

When we are inconvenienced or made uncomfortable for any reason, could we interrupt our automatic responses to feel singled out by misfortune? Most likely, we won't be able to do this easily, but as deep friends we can help each other.

The mind has such good arguments to keep us in old juicy patterns of victimization. But we always have the option to lean into Spirit. There we help one another see beyond our little context to a greater sense of things.

Forgetful and entrenched in habits as we are, we can be nudged back into living from the core and the cure—Spirit wrapping us with constant presence.

COMMUNITY

As loving friends, we are mirrors of compassion for each other, reflecting the joy and ache of being the ones we have been given to be. And we can also be those selfsame mirrors reflecting compassion for our immediate worlds of family and community. Most of us cannot range much further.

We know from science, however, that we exist in a unified field. Since this is so, what is done in love and awareness, though it may be small and local, impacts the whole. We can practice close to home with that understanding, offering that which is ours to do while knowing that it spreads in mysterious ways beyond our small circumstances.

The need for inclusion, understanding, remembrance, and support is continuous. Together with a heart's friend it is easier to respond to community needs, and to bring our compassion into concrete action.

Compassion can be so powerful for some people that they are willing to risk their lives. Perhaps we can risk more time, more of our financial resources, more of our skills because we are inwardly moved. To reflect one another's passion for the aches in the world is central in a serious friendship. We see how we each love—how we each *must* love.

If we are not drawn to the same endeavors, we can nevertheless know the feeling of the heart's pull and that nothing of love is ever lost. Once given, it continues though we may never know exactly how.

If challenge, suffering, and joy are the bricks, then compassion is the mortar that holds things together and creates structures in which we can live. That mortar must be mixed every day to be usable. It must be applied without pity or carelessness, but with loving attention. Compassion is a balm. It teaches balance. It gives us companionship and community.

As we experience it, we become more ourselves. Real empathy has no strategy, no sense of personal gain. It simply is. Mixed with the living water from our hearts, it can be liberally used wherever it is needed to hold what must be held.

In compassion we are the givers, the gift, and the receivers all at once. It takes place simultaneously everywhere. Even now, we are receivers of compassion given by others from distant places and other times.

Respect

How many marriages, partnerships, and friendships flounder because there is a basic lack of respect between the partners? All respect that is conditional—that is given because someone is attractive, smart, helpful, earns a great salary, has wonderful connections, dresses well, is wealthy, and so on—is respect that, in the final analysis, is based on function rather than on essence. These qualities are nice, of course, and we are often initially drawn to a person because of them. But these functions can start to feel old and be less and less important. We long to be respected for the one we essentially are, not for what we can provide.

Respect has to do with character, with presence and trustworthiness. It is our service to life itself that shines through even when our limitations are obvious. When we come to know that our essential value is not in question, we then receive our being as a gift beyond price, and we understand that it will take our whole lifetime to return that gift. How can respect be absent from this?

CONSIDERATION

We know respect isn't dumb awe of another. Respect is a dynamic, mutual condition in which both people can experience themselves as worthy of deep consideration. There are so many ways to respect another person. Could we notice the people we pass in the street, the people who help us with ordinary tasks—the clerk at the bank, the man who delivers fuel to the house, the waitress, the dental assistant...and so on?

A first respectful act is to be aware of these people, period—to see *them*. The second act would be to recognize that they belong, as we do, to the family of humanity. In a very short time, ordinary transactions carry an unspoken quality of courtesy.

Living this way, we would take out of our engagements the tendency to treat each other as functions rather than as people. Any time we do that, we've lost respect for ourselves without knowing it. We become more efficient and less humane. We demand and expect instead of request and receive. Our act of demanding makes us exploitative when the very same transactions we have many times a day could be between two equal humans.

What about this in our friendships? How often do we have hidden expectations of ourselves and of each other? These expectations carry silent demands. This is slippery territory. We harm our true connection in mazes of disregard and assumptions when we forget that every person is far more than the roles they fulfill. We are each of infinite value.

Though we fall into unconscious disregard now and then, who would be better to learn with than our friend who already appreciates our value? Simply that we are *is of benefit and beauty. We are each unique and sacred truths. The very least measure of respect we give to one another is to know this.*

When film is developed, the image forms gradually on the paper in the developing fluid until it is there in bright detail. Mutual respect is like developing fluid. Little by little we see each other more vividly and realize how holy and fragile our particularity is. We are here for such a very short time.

SERVICE

Another part of mutual respect is to confirm that Life is working on itself in each of us. We may be privileged by a close friendship to have a glimpse of what that may be, but we will never fully penetrate the mystery of it. We are each an alchemical vessel where meaning is taking place. We are formed and reformed by life, and Spirit is at work within us.

We are not only the place where Spirit is at work, but we are also that which is being worked. Therefore, we cannot *from the outside* presume to know what ultimately is being formed. We can only watch, wait, and wonder as the mystery takes place in us and between us.

Just as we would not, except in deep ignorance, invade and take over a service of worship that we might be attending, so also, if we understand a human life to be a service of worship, we should not enter another's sacred ritual with our own notions of *what should take place.*

Spirit asks us to be particular and distinct but being unique is not a license to have our way or to not be in cooperation. On the contrary, it is only as unique beings that a vital relationship becomes possible. We absolutely need the *otherness* of the other.

So it is that when we watch, wait, and wonder with the friend of our heart, we are in a kind of holy service. We can sense that we are actually waiting upon Spirit in each other, and that makes us true servants of life.

Respect could be thought of as a dance where steps to music are taken together and apart, allowing the dancers freedom. We cannot dance with someone who steps on our toes or holds us so tightly that we can't breathe.

A dance can have contrapuntal aspects. It can be fast for one and slow for another at the same time and still be in rhythm. What lets us dance well together is taking each other into account.

On an actual dance floor, we notice where others might be headed. We do not hoard the floor. We can train ourselves to remember that relationships share an emotional dance floor.

When we take care of the relationship first, many ways to dance are possible. There is a flow we know to be respect made visible.

TRUST

When we stand outside of our deep friendships for a moment and look in on the dancers, we would surely see the gestures, steps, and patterns of each of us and how they coincide. We would see the whole gestalt between the dancers. Watching we would recognize that the dancers have given themselves to their inner music and to the dance as well as to each other. If as deep friends we give ourselves to spiritual consciousness, there is a commitment present that is beyond the personal which then holds both our individual and our mutual movements in life.

There will be many times when we do not understand something one of us says or does. Yet when we respect that we are committed to Spirit, we can allow much though it may appear strange to us. We listen for the sacred tune in the other. We trust that Spirit is making music in each of us. We learn to trust that fact as much as we trust one another.

Many things come into our lives that we do not want to dance with, yet often those discordant melodies are part of completeness. We are not to live without challenges—rather we are to dance *with* them—not *to* them.

When we respect that our friends have given themselves to their inner music as we have done, we can better hold any difficulties, confusions, or misunderstandings we might have. We continue dancing together through both suffering and bliss.

How wordless music is! We are drawn by it into reveries and moods of all kinds. Our friendships, too, are held in a kind of vibration, a heavenly frequency.

It's not hard to sense a vibe in a moment in time or in the atmosphere of a room. We call them good vibes or bad vibes. We don't have to explain what we mean. We simply feel them.

Heavenly sounding is more difficult to name. It requires that we go into depths beyond what we know and can name, beyond our likes and dislikes, our habits and preferences. Spirit asks us to be connected beyond differences. There are no explanations, no analyses, nor any ways that can be spelled out for the way Spirit vibrates within us.

We must simply respect that this interior music simply is and let the connections beyond understanding move us into more and more meaningful ways to dance with life.

LIMITATION

An area more difficult perhaps than others, but nevertheless vital, is to respect our own and our beloved's limitations. We can grow. We can change. We can mature and deepen. A classical and difficult way to do this is to respect our limits.

It is within the limits of a bowl that something can be held. Going beyond those limits spills the contents. This is true for us as well. Respecting our limits, we can begin to care for them. Right there, on the edge of what we are and can do at any given time, we encounter the necessity of limits. Whole worlds exist precisely at such junctures.

Respecting our limits we become liminal—dwellers in that space where the known and the unknown meet, where the darkness of life and the light of life intermingle, where Spirit moves us because we have softened enough to accept our limitations and yet opened enough to not be defined by them. Just there, in that paradox, we are surely met by love. And just there, we can give each other the immense gift of spaciousness.

When we do not fight with the limitations of our beloved friends (perceived from our perspective, of course), and they do not fight with our limitations (perceived from their perspective), we have grace and space. When we do not fight with ourselves either, because of where we are and what we can and cannot do, we enter the depths of transformation. Trust is made visible, and humility is born—that quiet agent of possibility and hard-won peace.

Day after day as we age, we will know limitations of all kinds. Day after day these limits can help us grow in spiritual ways. Perhaps we become more loving, more patient, more tolerant of differences, more aware of what we want to give and more able to discern what no longer belongs.

We help each other see the best uses of our present abilities. We help each other sense the small, doable ways we are able to give of ourselves even as we diminish.

A limitation is always both an end and a beginning. It is a place to learn about love. Without our limitations, we would not be ourselves. All of us long to be loved as we are with our limits. And isn't that the limitless way that Spirit loves us even now?

PRESENCE

To be deeply respectful of another we must first be respectful of ourselves. We are each an unfinished work in progress. There is always a place we can improve. But becoming excellent, good or fault-free is not the goal, though we might have erroneously been taught that in our youth.

Not defined by our goals, we can become more self-respecting. Think of how many ways our egos are negotiating for a place to be okay. If only we could lose those ten pounds…if we could only get that job, or have that relationship…if only we were accepted by that group of powerful people…and so on. All that striving is striving for our own conditional respect. It's important to know that self-respect and self-love are vastly different. It is possible to have the one without the other.

Our goals are not the culprit. We need them to get anything done, but when we use them as the currency of self-respect, we are using them in the wrong way. Could we instead become more present? Could we meet our joy, our despair, our confusion, our anger and our silliness without disapproval *or* approval? Could we show up and not dismiss or disparage ourselves or make more of ourselves than we are?

Being present for just what is true is the most respectful we can be. We can safely go to the limit on that one! Able to show up as we truly are for our inner life's sake, would we not be more able to be present to one dear to our heart?

We do not learn best by fear, by avoidance, or by pleasing, but by trial and error, by discovery and surprise. We navigate best by simple recognition rather than by disapproval. Quirk by quirk we go—like steering south-by-southeast.

Mutual respect requires consideration, trust, and presence. It reaches us less in applause and approval than by the acceptance of our limitations and differences—the whole and unvarnished truth about us. That is respect that we can believe in.

In owning our beauty and our less than best, we are given a chance to experience that we are already loved and accepted by God and that God uses even our limping in good ways.

Self-Acceptance

Self-approval and self-acceptance are very different. In self-approval we get check marks for the good we think we do, for the fine impressions we think we make. There is a kind of tallying of merit that happens—so many good marks and we can earn our own conditional approval.

But in self-acceptance there is no tally sheet. There are no check marks. There is, instead, an inner transparency. We own how we project on others what we have not yet worked through in ourselves. We are aware of how we resist knowing the ways we hide so that we can feel what we call safe. We confess both our beauty and our faults and are open to forgiveness. Worthiness then comes to us as a matter of course. We do not earn it. It is a given we can humbly accept as fundamental and true.

PROJECTION

It's hard to respect and love another fully until we respect and love ourselves. This is an obvious truth, but hard to live. As much as we may want to love our heart's friend with complete freedom and depth, we may not be able to. Aspects of ourselves that we have not yet learned to know and love into healing and maturity get in the way.

It is usually in the deep loves of our lives that pockets of unworthiness surface. The very safety of love seems to give permission for that which is unloved to emerge. When we are safe, open, and vulnerable, we are also easily reinjured.

As loving friends, we try to see each other as well as we can, but we are destined to be faulty witnesses from time to time. The parts we enjoy, admire, and are happy about are what attract us to each other. We sense an affinity with what we see either because we have it as a capacity as well, or we have it as a potential to be developed.

When we find ourselves in criticism, disappointment, anger, and confusion, we have run into a negative projection of some kind. No matter how we were provoked, we have nevertheless found a pocket of unworthiness that belongs to us to work on.

Side by side, we can witness and be part of a rich process of growing. Ultimately, we are responsible for ourselves. Coming into wholeness is our soul's task and ours alone.

Whatever can develop in our soul is ours to help cultivate, but it is not ours to determine. Each of us will always be in progress—called into deeper truthfulness and humility. We live in a mystery—one we cannot fully understand. We each carry an abyss of separateness, a loneliness in which and through which we can come to wholeness and to God. As deep friends, we see each other off into the inner wilderness.

The necessity for alone time is real, and it becomes blessed into solitude by Spirit—not by our actions or our talking. In that silence—alone with aloneness—another reality takes over. Projection shrinks and we perceive one another as part of God.

RESISTANCE

Learning self-acceptance is one insult after the other. In contrast, self-knowledge is easier, for it is information *about* oneself. But it is not acceptance. We all have interior reservations—many we are unaware of. These reservations shape our stance in life. To surrender to the truth of them when there is no one to hold us, is chilling.

We resist in so many ways. We judge, demand, argue, control, and insist that we, and others, should be different than they are or than we are. We often do this subtly, but we are doing it, nevertheless. Listening to any ordinary conversation reveals how often we think we know best. We may also space out, occupying ourselves in countless ways, many of them even useful. We are resisting by default, distracted by things that are not fundamental to us. Or we distract ourselves with illusions, making ourselves seem important and entitled, or making others out to be so.

We cling to things as well; things we believe will *do it* for us. We grasp after acknowledgement, persons, circumstances, and things we think will enhance us. Ultimately, no outward thing will do it for us.

It is in solitude that we come to know the countless ways we resist. Alone we have a chance to hold hands with our avoidance and face the truth that we are essentially powerless. Befriending powerlessness is a royal road. The sovereignty found there will not be taken from us.

Alone in a wild place in nature most of us feel small. The empty sky appears enormous, the dark night endless, the forest impenetrable. Inner places can feel the same to us. Our thoughts tangle and twist us into all kinds of wilderness. Our imaginations exaggerate the difficulties we must face.

These are the dark nights. We are trapped in the jungle of confusion, alone in an arid desert of anger or a swamp of grief. We want to run away from experiencing any of it, or we want to fight with it to the bitter end. A deeper truth is there also—that we are, and have been, fundamentally naked and powerless all along, yet we belong to the whole—to God's huge inclusiveness. And we are worthy of care.

CONFESSION

In time, we find that all the ways of avoiding our inner truth do not work. We sense that we are living in the scaffolding of resistance and insistence, not in the solid home of self-acceptance. Scaffolding is important when we are repairing a building, but it is in the way when we want to live in it.

Acceptance is not approval. It is bigger than that. Approval gives a positive focus, but a focus, nevertheless. It is pinpointing. Acceptance gives us space as wide as the sky and renders approval unimportant. Neither is acceptance agreement. Though pleasing, agreement is also limiting.

Acceptance appears docile, but it is the opposite. It is dynamic and inclusive. It offers space without capitulation. It is, in fact, confession. We cannot have acceptance without confession. When our faults are truly confessed, we have accepted their existence. Curiously, it is then they seem to shrink, and they come into a new proportion. Less judged and resisted, they change and diminish accordingly. We find that, in essence, they were thwarted desires that needed to be filled in better ways.

Confessed, our beauty and goodness change also. They grow, and with more room we often find we have talent for things we were not aware of. We may also dare things that might not work for us but are worth the trying. Without judgment hounding us into tight corners, we expand and experiment. Living in self-acceptance, we live in an ongoing confession, a home with many doors and windows that invites the world to live *with* us.

When we first move into the home of self-acceptance, it is usually a small place—maybe just a little study in which to be cozy now and then. As we acknowledge the truth about ourselves, we learn that this home has doors with no locks, that there are rooms within it that we didn't know were there—rooms for us to make our own.

Acceptance grows in the light of confession and experience. Room upon room continues to open. There are always new chambers to find and to live in. Slowly we understand that this home, which we believed to be small is really a mansion with space for everything. Acceptance is the longed-for home of the heart.

FORGIVENESS

It is not enough to know that we said or did something that hurt us or another. The acceptance of the facts is essential. So is the acceptance of our regrets and our self-judgments about what happened. These are the preambles of forgiveness. Even though we understand *all of that*, to experience that we are forgiven is a deeper matter.

We can't *do* forgiveness. It is something that *is done* in us. To forgive and to be forgiven is a mystery we open to. We cannot force it or manufacture it in any way. To experience remorse is a needed step. It is a beginning. To continue to be remorseful over and over is actually a kind of pride. We are the judge, the jury, and the convict. By being right about how wrong we are, we are still playing God.

If we are to give or to receive forgiveness, we must turn toward the source of forgiveness. It is in the mystery of God's love that our self-betrayals and failures find rest. It is in Love's deep embrace that we wait. It is a profound silence where our shame can be transformed.

We will never be fully conscious of what transpires in that unfathomable stillness. But we can entrust ourselves to it. We can attend it with our whole being and lean into it. In time, we may see signs of release. Old pain leaves the cells of our bodies and dissolves. We feel lighter. Muted like an old photograph, the past grows soft around the edges. It is another dawn in which we see light around old issues and the glimmer of new beginnings.

We sit by the door of silence with our old familiars—shame and remorse. Though we do many outward things in the world, we are secretly sitting in front of that closed door for days, months, and years. We are waiting on love.

We don't know if the door will ever open. Yet if we persist and sit with longing, we can feel that under our failures is our own love that calls to the Love behind the silence.

One day, the door opens on its own and we step over the threshold filled with the Presence that waited with us on both sides of the door.

WORTHINESS

Our worthiness is there from the beginning. We have simply forgotten that we entered life trailing clouds of glory, and that when we depart, all we have learned of love will be our passport. Worthiness is a wondrous thing. It is softer than skin and holds the knowledge that all is gift—our lives, our opportunities, and even our suffering. Worthiness was given to us with our first breath. We need only to draw another breath to recall that we are inspired ones.

Breath by breath we are to give away everything we have received. This is not poverty. It is the wealth of self-expression. In sharing our gifts, they multiply, and we become ourselves more and more. However small our offerings may seem to us, there are countless ways these gifts are received. We will not know the full extent of this.

Does a tree know who or what benefits from the oxygen it produces? It must give to be alive. We, too, must give to be alive. When we don our worthiness the way leaves clothe a tree or the stars bespangle the sky, we are clothed in a mantle of grace. We own the preciousness of our lives and know them to be treasures, ones we have a lifetime to share.

A new day begins when we consciously wake to the holy worth of our life. We wash our faces with the air of morning. Having confessed our projections, our resistance, and our need for forgiveness, we can take up the work of our hands with a sense of wonder—that we are continually forgiven and have a part to play—a way to serve the larger purpose.

Living this awareness, we confirm and enlarge the wonder. Day after day we spend ourselves. Even when we are old and can only smile and breathe, our worth extends into hidden places beyond our knowing. Our worth is not ours. It belongs to life. We are life's treasures and of infinite value.

Longing

There is always longing going on within us. We are born with desires: first for food, safety, and emotional connection. As infants, we reach into life with those drives. As vulnerable as we are, the desire to live and have our needs met is a fierce one that far outweighs our size.

Later in life our deep longings are often felt more diffusely. They may even be obscure or dulled. We have vague sensations that hint that we have more possibilities than we are living. These hints are nudges from the beyond within. The unknown beckons. We feel a fearful kind of excitement.

Since we cannot go where we have not imagined, we need dreams. Without dreams our souls shrivel. We need images of what might be possible for us, icons that inspire us onward. We need our deep friends to believe that we can achieve the longings of our heart. We need to believe that Spirit wants our passion to be made visible for our own sake and for the sake of all that is.

POSSIBILITIES

By embracing our worth, we also touch our deep longings. On a spiritual level, we know we are called to be something for all of existence, however humble that might be. This calling is like a seed and has great vitality. It waits inside sometimes for decades, and it needs our engagement to be lived.

Hints about this calling come to us in ordinary ways though they are often ignored. We do not realize that they point to something larger—a possibility that is unique to us and ours to develop. Our friends can help us notice these hints and to act on them. There is an impulse-logic to them that is dynamic. We must not think of these nudges as irrelevant nonsense, impulsivity, or ego gratification. These nudges lie deep within. They ask us to feel, to engage, and to commit to action on behalf of our essence. They never have *profit* or *self-enhancement* as a primary objective. They are simply asking for soil so they can grow and be expressed. A heart's friend can give us support to engage our longing.

It is from these levels that people will give their lives for another, spend years in causes they believe in, enter experiences very different from what they have previously known, and create beauty and meaning where there was none before. When our seed longings are nudged and given encouragement from a true friend, we can feel how everything inside wants to say *yes.*

We may in quiet, in conversation, or even in passing, sense that something is awake within us. We may feel it when we hear a certain kind of music. A painting may sweep us into its beauty. The smooth working of a machine may enthrall us. A thorny problem lures us into puzzling. We are triggered and filled with vitality.

Hints come unexpectedly, and often in undramatic ways. They nudge an inner capacity that is unique to us and ours to develop. As loving friends, we can be aware that soul seeds lie fallow and dormant within us. Together we can challenge and help each other dare to find ways to live them.

FEARS

When we were young, we may have played dare you to gain the courage to do something we were afraid to do. Dare you to jump in the water. Dare you to climb over the fence. Dare you to open the cellar door and go down in the dark. We were dealing with childhood fears. As adults, we still deal with fear. To dare to act on our deep desires can still feel like jumping in the water and not knowing how deep it is.

As adults, our fears are less about physical safety. We fear looking stupid. We fear failing at what we try or finding that what we desired isn't what it's cracked up to be. We fear we've no talent for those things for which we long.

Fear is loud and has many voices. It keeps saying *what if* and lists all the negative outcomes we could imagine. But with a true friend, we can listen to another voice saying *what if*—a voice that imagines possibility.

What if you try to draw and paint as you have always longed to do? What if you take an art class? What if you doodled every day for the sheer fun of it? What if you make your own greeting cards? What if you are not a graphic artist but have fun trying? What if, since you love color and form, you make beauty every day as you build or garden or set the table or arrange your tools? What if beauty is what you are, and these are small but significant ways you can recognize this truth.

Playing what if with the friend of our heart, we are watering our seed longings, helping them to shed their shells, to open, and to take root.

Over time we come to know where we limp and where we soar, and what unnecessary cages we live in from which we long to be free. When we intuit for each other, we are playing what if. Imagined possibilities fly between us. They are playful suggestions that do not demand an outcome. We are simply asking each other to think in winged ways.

When one of those insights resonates with us, we feather out and feel graced. It may be that particular inspiration that allows us to let go of fear and to fly.

DREAMS

When we buy vegetable or flower seeds, we get them in packets with pictures and planting instructions. We know what to expect when the seeds germinate. Soul seeds don't come with instructions or guaranteed outcomes. Following our deep desires, we live by trial and error, not by trial and perfect. Errors are part of our journey. Once embraced, they have a chance to be changed into blessings.

Because we don't know what kind of seeds we have inside, we must cultivate them to recognize them. Even with insight, we don't get a sense of the whole or of how very disparate things might be brought together. Here our heart's friend is so very helpful. When we are afraid, we encourage each other to remember that uncertainty is the birthplace of courage. We remind each other that certainty is a closed book; uncertainty allows for possibility. We hold one another's errors lightly, knowing they are detours that will eventually take us around to where we can continue our journey.

Helping each other dream, we water, feed, and protect one another from wind and harsh rain. We look for little green shoots in spring and remember that germination times can be slow and that all the right circumstances of weather and nutrients must be there for green shoots to emerge. We know all work in manifestation is the work of human love joined to the Great Love that always creates with us.

Dreaming forward—what is it but the careful use of all senses plus a sixth? It is a kind of Braille. We are feeling our way—sensing and pausing—not hurrying—intimately touching the next possibility with thought and care.

When we go at that loving pace, we are less likely to dream wrongly. We will be informed—one hand tracing the page of life, the other giving support. Our hearts already know something our lives must discover, or perhaps it is we who are the ones being discovered? Can we really know if we are doing the dreaming, or if we are being dreamed?

IMAGES

We cannot go where we have not imagined. We need representations of our dreams, to feel them, sense them, and clothe them with outward visible signs of our inward longing. Desires that are deeply pictured and bodily felt are prayers in and of themselves. Aristotle said that "the soul never thinks without an image." Picturing our deep longings with a special friend is a prayer doubled. To picture is not just visual. Some people hear their images, feel them as sensation, or experience them in other ways.

However it happens, our deep desires move into being when we embrace the images that represent them. They are icons of power and work inside us in mysterious ways.

The longing for inner freedom, for instance, is a bodily sensation, an emotional reality, and a way of living in the world. A photo of a dancer in the ecstasy of dance might be an icon for that longing. Looked at daily, it is a form of motivation as well as a visual prayer.

The desire to be more centered might be a beautiful calligraphy of a circle or a tree. To be of service may be imaged as a pair of open hands. We help each other by looking for the right images. Strangely, once our longings are embraced, it's not unusual for the perfect images to arrive at our doorsteps as if by magic. Spirit enters the unconscious using these guiding icons and awakens their possibility in us. Using them, we develop a stronger and stronger disposition toward our hearts' desires and for ways to live them.

We would not have found a soul-guiding image unless we were ready for it. The seeds of our longing wait as all seeds do for the right time and the right conditions. With our heart's friend, we can better trust ourselves to wait.

When we wait upon something, we serve it and anticipate it. It is a deeply creative process. When we have waited on an image long enough, it is integrated and becomes just an ordinary picture again. The sparkle it held for us is now inside. We are ready for another image to show us where to grow. There is no end to this growth as long as we are alive.

FRUITION

We desire many outward things that we believe will make our lives richer and more joyous. They may be jobs, partners, homes, fame, fun, wealth, adventure, and so on. Underneath these desires are the deeper longings: yearning for time, for soulful relatedness, for peace, for simplicity, for meaningful service, for self-expression and beauty. We want to be open and inclusive. We want to be present to life, to be its lovers. We are to fulfill that mandate abundantly—to have life and to be life. And we are not alone in wanting this fruition. Spirit works with us to bring our deep desires into being.

Sometimes they can only come to us through suffering. Suffering redirects us from paths that do not lead to our deepest longings. Illness may bring with it the time we have yearned for. Lost love may bring us into greater self-love. Peace may come to us when we give up false effort around things that can never bring us peace. Loss of work may lead us to paths that have service as their essence. Through suffering, we may learn to value small, significant things we never valued before. Something we can be sure of is that God's love is at work in the depth of our longing.

This yearning never ends. It is a red thread imbedded in our lives—an artery. To stop yearning is to be bloodless. Spirit seeks Itself in us. We cannot be without longing. As heart friends, we know that what we deeply yearn for is what Spirit longs for within us.

Serving the deep longings of our being we hold each other to the central task of our lives—to embody our core. Despite the fears we might have, we look for possibilities and guiding images. We dream each other forward and do not skip over the small, radiant chances to love, to notice, and to help.

When we create something new, we are aware that we are that place where Love is working on itself to bring about fruition. Serving our soul's longing, we know it to be praise.

Loving

To love and be loved is a longing that we all have. The way love reaches us is different for each of us, and how deeply we allow it to enter us is a lifetime's work.

We are nourished and shaped by human love or lack of it, but we are rendered whole by the love Spirit has for us. It is there that all we are and all we can become are held in infinite tenderness and compassion. How we arrive at knowing this and feeling it as true for us is a central task of deep friendship. It is within a human framework of compassion and respect that we can begin to sense and eventually experience how Spirit yearns for us and for our wholeness.

We give each other loving awareness, and it leads us in time to the Presence, to Spirit, our deepest friend.

CONFIDENCE

In a deep friendship, we have those fertilizing moments when something is mutually confirmed. This recognition is a place of germination—a place brought to life by the presence of the other. We keep alive the truest parts of each other—that edge of growth where both excitement and necessity come together. At that convergence, there is a dynamic energy that does not want to be denied.

How do we love this way? We know by now that we do so first by recognition, but we also do so by a visceral trust that the other will be true to his or her edge of possibility. It is an instinctual faith in each other's courage and tempo. Where we might experience urgency or reluctance, our friend will remind us that Spirit is at work in us, that growth happens in many curious ways—sometimes allowing periods of rest, or periods in which we suffer adversity, or even periods of wallowing in discouragement.

Visceral trust is not a thought. It's not prayer. It's a certitude—a bit like a lighted window in the dark. We are awake on each other's behalf even if one of us is plodding through the most tangled undergrowth in some wood too far away for any light to be seen.

We are not rescued by our heart's friend so much as *awaited* in trust and confidence.

To be viscerally trusted is to shine a light as much for ourselves as for the other. We are most loving toward one another by being constant in our own growing. In saying yes to this vulnerable and dynamic level of being—living it ourselves and encouraging our heart's friend to live it also—we form a matrix of light and strength that we can both rely on.

It is an experience of Spirit's invisible net of love in which we are held always. When our very cells trust Spirit's work within us, it will not only have been yesterday, it will also be yes/today.

EMBRACING *ALL OF IT*

Love is paradoxical. On the one hand, we know each other deeply, and on the other hand, we know that we cannot ever know each other completely. We live love by a continual repeated, mutual discovery of one another. Over and over in countless ways, we find love for our heart's friend in small gestures of care and in the most ordinary details of connection. It is here that we learn to open to the context of the one we love.

A fish is not alive without water, nor is a bird alive without air. As humans, our air and water are the elements that have shaped us. We come to be ourselves within the various contexts of family, school, friends, interests, work, and even landscapes. We have a vast network of associations in which we are embedded—some wonderful and some that are fraught with terrible difficulty. Loving another in depth, we must also embrace their context.

At the beginning of a friendship, we may not realize that we are to be open to the whole field in which our friends have become who they are. Love asks us to embrace each other with all that made us and keeps us.

Embracing *all of it* is very difficult. We want to eliminate parts we don't like and add other parts. We want to determine what our mutual meaning should be. But all such efforts at control and manipulation will fail. Slowly, we learn to let Spirit be the largest, mutual context.

We are always engaged in the beloved or feared things of our past. They are part of us and seek love from us and love from someone whom we trust. All of it wants inclusion.

Gradually, we learn to care about the things that are meaningful to our heart's friends—both the longed for things and the feared things. And we support our friends to love what they already love.

More and more we can be "for" one another without strings attached. Embodying this willingness is never finished. It must be lived daily. Neither is the process about ultimate success, but about the humility that accepts failure and begins again and again.

CONSCIENCE

There is another meaningful way that deep friends love. Not only do we come to more consciousness together, but we also come to conscience. Being aware is good in and of itself, but knowing that we know, or shall we say knowing *with* our friend (*con siencia*) establishes us in a truth from which we cannot hide.

We are not loved in a conscience way by many people or very often. How profound is the love that a person gives when he or she respectfully acts to further our conscience! Deep friends can call one another's deceptions and half lies. Where we often weasel out of knowing what we know alone, it's impossible to do so in the context of committed friendship. The truth is written in the heart and mind of our friend as well as in our own heart and mind. It becomes shared truth and therefore a sacred trust.

There are so many layers to us humans, and those areas of shame and fear, of injury and distrust as well as the areas of soul beauty and competence are the very ones we protect and hide. Knowing that we know them, and knowing that our beloved friend also knows them, allows us access in a new way. We can bear their truth in all senses of that word.

It is not surprising, then, that many companionships do not blossom into deep friendships because it takes such courage and responsibility to act as a loving conscience for and with another person. It may be here that most people are deeply alone.

As solemn as this mutual task is, we can be light about it all. Making fun of our selves or each other is that feather's loving touch of humor that lets us be amused by our own ridiculousness, our habits of avoidance and subterfuge. Then, what is heavy to bear can be brought to right proportion.

Laughter can be the recognition of the tragic and impossible seen from a startling angle, making it suddenly not only possible, but perhaps even human, funny, and lovable. In the throes of a great guffaw, our tears run and our bellies dance. A big laugh is like a sob. We are crying and tickled pink at the same time. In laughter, we are shaken free and so revivified into hopefulness and wholeness again.

SHARED WORK

It is by the shining interior light of our friendship that we illumine more than our own concerns. It follows that the love in a deep friendship naturally spills out into shared work in the world.

That does not mean that we do the same work necessarily, though it may sometimes be so. Rather, we are supported by each other's journeys to give ourselves more fully to others in our own way. The confluence of our shared enthusiasm and mutual interest in being of service becomes an energy field that allows us to explore and risk more. By learning with each other, we find the courage to step over the invisible lines that we draw in our native caution.

To take up our purpose in the world together is powerful. It is like gardening. Pruning, turning over new soil, feeding, and replanting are always there in life. As friends, we will know what condition our soil is in, what it can bear, what it needs, what season it is in life, and where support should be given. Through mutual awareness we participate in one another's work in the world, and it becomes one shared work.

We help each other avoid many spiritual traps. One trap is feeling that we do things all by ourselves. We never do. Spirit is working for us all the time and often through the love of a friend.

We will also avoid being possessive about accomplishments. We move from self-congratulation to the wonder of feeling that something has been done that is of value.

Our work in the world may be in the same place or in separated locations and about different concerns. Yet the harvest is communal. It feeds us both and many others. As deep friends, we help each other garden our lives for the sheer privilege of doing so.

We know that love is not something we do, but something we are given to be.

KNOWING NOTHING

Writing about love is very difficult. We know so little about it, confusing need and fuzzy feelings for an experience that is both as familiar as the smell of our child's skin and as strange and invisible as the floor of the ocean. We know nothing really, and that is essentially a comforting place to both begin and to continue.

Knowing nothing, we can relax and be foolish. Knowing nothing is at least a truth we can embrace. No doubt we will find how fickle we are when only feelings determine our way. Like New England weather, feelings change continually. We love and yet often we disparage what we love. We are proud of those we love, and yet we seem to require that they be more than they can be or different than they are.

To love with any constancy and fullness of heart is not something we do; it is done in us by Love itself. Taken by surprise, even after years of loving someone or something, we find ourselves in love with them again. We surrender to the recognition of something internal that is also externally there in living color.

Deep friends actually fall in love with Spirit as we perceive it embodied in each other. It is felt by some as a kind of recognition "from before" or "from forever and always." We know yet have no way to know how and why we know it. That brings us full circle to knowing nothing, yet feeling how Spirit is with us in conscience and confidence and shares the work of loving *all of it*.

When we have the magic of knowing without knowing, we enter the world in participation instead of observation. It is like walking in a landscape and feeling it around us instead of flying over it in a plane or whizzing past it on a train. We escape our closed compartments, our sealed windows, and our habitual speed.

It is then that we discover ourselves on sturdy ground where everything becomes both a self-discovery and an us-discovery. Then the held hand of the other is of such necessary beauty that we could never take it for granted. We would not know who was holding whose hand. In that shared landscape, if someone called us by Love's name, we would both answer.

Last Word

To have a heart's friend and to be a heart's friend is to have a blessing and to be a blessing. I cannot think of anything more sustaining that helps us grow in every way, including spiritually. By such communion, we become more than we could ever be alone. As Robert Louis Stevenson said, "*A friend is a gift you give yourself.*"

If, however, there is no one in your life presently that can serve in that capacity, please remember that Spirit is already there as your friend and accompanies you always. You can commune with Spirit and find that by listening with your heart you will hear, on an inner level, how Spirit holds you, guides you, and loves you.

In a deep friendship, we create a sanctuary where something dynamic can happen. It is a place of giving and receiving without strings, with no motivation to be "something" or "someone"—we simply offer ourselves in faith to one another. This giving has a quality of vulnerability and naked transparency. When such a gift of self is truly given and received, we meet as equals and are touched, confirmed, and enlarged.

Together this way, we stop searching and are found instead in the mystery of God who made us for life and for each other. There we experience a joy which does not hesitate in the face of circumstance—be it uncertainty, suffering, fear, or celebration—but rather encircles us and allows us to open to all we can be.

How mysterious is love.
It binds us close to one another
even as it gives us freely back to ourselves.

Praise for *Deep Friendship*

"Gunilla Norris has gifted us with a marvelous little book on creating and nurturing authentic friendships. Read this book slowly—like a prayer book. The poetry of her words will bless you with every page turn. *Deep Friendship* sings of a resilient faith lifted out of the dance of life. I fully recommend it."

—Macrina Wiederkehr, OSB, retreat guide and author of *Abide: Keeping Vigil with the Word of God*

"*Deep Friendship* is an invitation. Here Norris invites the reader to explore what it is to have and what it is to be a friend of depth—of the soul. In a café, at bedside, under a favorite tree, this little book can become a deep friend, guiding you into a more intimate relationship with your self and the world. Respond with the word *yes*."

—Jamie Reaser, author of *Sacred Reciprocity*

"In her graceful, elegant, and pensive writing style, Gunilla Norris muses on the incomparable treasures of deep friendship. She mines the spiritual depths of this intimate relationship and challenges us to open ourselves fully to its emotional radiance and precious beauty. In these times of increasing social isolation, we all need to be nurtured by steady friends who are with us for the long haul."

—Frederic Brussat, co-author of *Spiritual Literacy*

"Like a master diamond cutter, Norris deftly works her words to reveal the myriad facets of the mystery of sacred friendship in all its grace and durability. What she offers are the luminous contours of life's most precious gem, whose worth is beyond calculation, whose every feature refracts not just light, but enlightenment."

—Kathleen Noone Deignan, the founding director of the Deignan Institute for Earth and Spirit at Iona University